MW01539278

THIS JOURNAL BELONGS TO:

110 Page | 6”x9” | Blank Lined Journal

Made in the USA
Las Vegas, NV
21 December 2021

39121081R00061